THE SYNDROME

One Bug, One Bite Will Change Your Life As You Know It

M. ADKINS

The Syndrome
One bug, one bite, will change your life
as you know it

E-book ISBN: 978-1-7353832-1-7

Print book ISBN: 978-1-7353832-0-0

Library of Congress Control Number: 2020918886

To my wife and children, Stacy, Silas, and Selah

CONTENTS

1 The Infection   Pg. 1

2 The Narcissist   Pg. 6

3 Planet Zit   Pg. 11

4 The Grand Negotiators   Pg. 14

5 Peer Pressure   Pg. 17

6 Birds and the Bees   Pg. 19

7 Somebody else's Problem   Pg. 21

8 Epilogue   Pg. 24

Author's Page   Pg. 32

"Simon felt a perilous necessity to speak; but to speak in assembly was a terrible thing to him. 'Maybe,' he said hesitantly, 'maybe there is a beast.

'Not surprisingly, the reaction from the other boys is outrageous laughter, but Simon tries again. 'What I mean is...maybe it's only us.'"

~ William Golding, Lord of the Flies ~

1 THE INFECTION

Webster's Encyclopedic Unabridged Dictionary of the English Language defines the word "syndrome" as a group of symptoms that together are characteristic of a specific condition, disease, or the like.

Teenagers live in a world of virtual reality, celebrity reality, abbreviated text messages, and urban vocabularies. As a parent, I wonder, "Does it ever end?" I always remember the words of Captain Barbosa of the first Pirates of the Caribbean movie, The Curse of the Black Pearl, "You best start believe in ghost stories because you're in one." In my case, it's a symbiotic relationship with a teenager who happens to be suffering from an insect venom-induced syndrome.

Exactly one week after my son's twelfth birthday, I started to notice subtle hints that something was wrong. Simple commands, such as "Take out the trash," "Put your dishes in the sink," and "Clean the litterbox" became unspeakable chores for him. The definitive response to my wife and I when requesting such tasks were met with a nonchalant, "I don't want to do it," and "My sister doesn't have to do this, so why should I?" In the beginning, there would be no eye contact. There was only a long pause and the expectation that as his parents, we'd better obey him or he could somehow dismiss us in some way as if we were his personal assistants.

When it first began, we shook our disapproving heads with a light giggle, then attended to the chores that needed attention. But, somewhere after the 4395th day of his birth, it became worse. Now the son, who is twelve-and- two-weeks-old, is glaring at his folks, ballin' his fists, puffing out his chest, and shaking his head at the parents who brought him into this world as if to say, "Do you hear me? Exactly! That's what I thought," when asked to do simple commands.

I had to assert myself as the head of the household, the great hunter and defeater of twelve-year-old boys, and move toward him with a glare in my eye that expressed an internal rage that has only been seen in horror movies. As I stood there, more than a foot taller than him, I reminded him of whose house he lived in, whose clothes he was actually wearing, and whose food he was enjoying when he got hungry. Also, I had to remind him of whose iPad and video game apps he was playing when he was given the right to play, not to mention whose TV he frequently relished over when his programming was on.

The next day, I woke at five o'clock in the morning, as I usually do on the weekends, to feed the pets and to have my morning coffee without any interruption, confrontation, or argument. As I sat on the sofa, I began to ponder the reasoning and the timing behind his unexplainable lack of respect, his disregard of authority, the constant rolling of the eyes and the screeching, crackling sound of his voice.

During spring recess, I remember distinctly, while picking my son and daughter up from their camp activities, they complained of insect bites. The bites were small, puffy, slightly reddish-pink colored, and very itchy. When we arrived home, my wife and I cleaned their wounds with hot, soapy water. Then we dried them and applied the usual anti-itch hydrocortisone ointment. We watched them closely for a few days to ensure they weren't dizzy or developed a fever due to the chemical reaction of the blood and venom that had transpired through their bodily fluid exchange. What if, though, the gestation process of his symptomatic condition, stemming from the insect bites, took longer—about a month or two to germinate. Normally, I would dismiss this type of thought process from my mind, but looking back, I realized now that his sport-playing mates were victims as well. For instance, one day, my wife and I were waiting at our son and daughter's team swim practice and were like the other parents there, waiting to retrieve their sons and daughters. We saw Mr. Brooks, always well-mannered, very sociable, and always well versed in past, present, and future sports events. Most parents enjoyed his company because when he was around, he broke up the monotony of just sitting and waiting on a pool deck. On this particular day, Mr. Brooks seemed to have enough of his daughter Margaret's haphazard response to "Let's go! I have an important meeting to attend." He shouted again, "Margaret, let's go! I have an important meeting to attend," but this time, with all three key ingredients: rage, feeling, and body-piercing anger. All the parents tried to ignore the sound and the direction from where it came, but just like a little fender-bender pulled over on the side of the road or police lights on, every one of the parents became like rubber-neckin' looky-loos and began to watch with an uncanny fascination. Mr. Brooks poured into her with a verbal jab that mirrored a hungry prizefighter setting up his opponent. He yelled, "Why are you inch-worming to the car with the dexterity of a lethargic sloth?" He screamed again at her, "When I said hurry up, that does not mean keep talking to your friends and act as if my meeting was not as important than you socializing with your so-called little clique. I put food on the table every night, I'm forty-five years old, I bought my own home. I take my family on vacation each year, and now I have a teenager who resembles my daughter telling me how high I'm supposed to jump. And trying to dictate where I can go. No, sir! Not on my watch! I say what else you got? For the last time, you better get your sassy self into my car in the next two minutes or we are going to have it out in front of your friends, missy."

Now earlier, I mentioned my ten-year-old daughter was bitten as well. Her symptoms at this time, although present, are inconsistent, to say the least, but when they materialize, they come in the form of mood swings, continual crying, and the silent treatment. They have been known to emerge after enduring insurmountable bouts of teasing, invasions of privacies, and lying about who did what and how. These bug bites can cause my daughter to come down with the crazies, mixed with a bit of anger and a splash of uncontrollable rage.

Case in point, since it is a dog eat dog world, we enrolled our son and daughter into martial arts. They studied Wing Chun, the art of Ip Man and Bruce Lee. After four years of Wing Chun, you would think my son would have learned a certain level of respect and discipline since the Sifus (teachers) have them mediate after each class and then give them a word of enlightenment verbally and on paper so they would not forget. One day, the Sifus started class with the word of enlightenment first. He looked at all the students intently as they all sat with their legs crossed in Lotus position and eyes affixed to them. The Sifus spoke in turn voicing, "Dirty Clothes," by Ajan Chah. "It is only natural that when we put on dirty clothes and our bodies are dirty that our minds, too, will feel uncomfortable and depressed. However, if we keep our bodies clean and wear clean, neat clothes, it makes our minds light and cheerful.

So, too when morality is not kept, our bodily actions and speech are dirty, and this is a cause for making the mind unhappy, distressed, and heavy. We are separated from practice and this prevents us from penetrating into the essence of ourselves. The wholesome bodily actions and speech themselves depend on the mind properly trained, since the mind orders body and speech. Therefore, we must continue to practice by training our minds." After, they instructed the group to work in pairs practicing attacks and defenses of Si Lim Tao, otherwise known as sticky hands technique. Naturally, our children wanted different training partners but the Sifus insisted they work together to learn how to respect one another.

As it was, my son was being extremely rough with my daughter, breaking through her defenses and slapping her in the face. The Sifus warned him not to make contact after he broke through her defense but as the old saying goes, "*boys *will be boys.*" With each slap, any observer could see the tension growing within my daughter's face. It was similar to watching a ripple in the ocean. As the wind picks up, the ripple begins to develop into a swell growing in size and in power. Soon after, the swell matures into a wave pushing towards the shore until it crashes down with a great rage, and the water expands angrily over the surface of the earth. Similarly, to the torrent of waters, my daughter, angrily broke through by son's guard with a savage rage and unleashed a fury of centerline punches to my son's chin knocking him off his feet with a loud THUD. As parents inhaled loudly, the Sifus rushed over to inquire about what had just happened and to check on the condition of my son. Embarrassed and red in the face, my son rose to his feet, and played down the success of her attack, by stating, he wasn't paying attention and watching what he was doing. Although that was the official statement, onlookers who were present know the truth. It was the crazies; anger with a splash of uncontrollable rage.

2 THE NARCISSIST

"I don't care what you think unless it's about me."

~ Kurt Cobain ~

Narcissism is defined as: 1. self- love; egocentrism 2. admiration of one's own physical or mental attributes.

Unlike the bites of a mosquito I mentioned earlier, where the bites are small, puffy, slightly reddish-pink color and very itchy, the incubation process in this stage leaves the victim developing an enlarged head, figuratively and symbolically. Although some parents have disagreed with this deduction and have argued that their children have become a casualty of the Shuar tribe of the Amazon from whence they have never traveled. *In case you are unfamiliar to the Shuar tribe, they were the indigenous group who supplied the demand for shrunken heads and shrunken brains in the 19th century.*

Another outstanding feature of this stage is the rancid aroma lingering throughout the air with their every move. As your infected teen prances in and out of different pathways that invade your direct vicinity, they are secreting pheromonic signals. To the laymen, these signals represent "B.O.," a.k.a. body odor. Usually, with one whiff of the scent, reminiscent of an overly ripe piece of fruit, parents storm the local store in a search of some type of deodorant. With the purchase of these pheromonic inhibitors, parents can begin to salvage hair follicles and bring back to life their nearly damaged nostrils from paralysis.

Besides, from the outset, teens begin to experience a type of psychological psychosis. A person agonizing with these symptoms will experience delusions, hallucinations, talking incoherently to others and themselves, frequent agitation, lying, and denial of their actions. The person with the condition usually isn't aware of their behavior or at least that's what they will say. For instance, have you noticed your son or daughter brushing their hair for hours at a time? Are they staring at themselves in the mirror, nodding and mumbling, saying something of the sort, "I look good," or "My body looks great," followed by a mix of project runway and bodybuilder poses, and then the utterance of "Everybody likes me." It reminds me of Rodney Dangerfield's movie Ladybugs where he states, "I'm great, I'm wonderful! Everybody likes me!" Thereafter, they are seen stumbling into your room in just their undergarments and begin to show you their backsides and asking for your opinion "Does my butt look too big? What about my quads? They are a nice size, aren't they?" as they stare back into your mirror. Furthermore, you may notice your adolescent walking by the mirror with their going-out clothing on, checking themselves out, how they look when they walk, still talking to themselves about "Should I have my hand in my pocket or out; should I wear a hat; should I have a serious face or a slight grin." You may also find them checking how they look from the backside, leaving the scene. And if you are misfortunate enough to catch a glimpse, they switch the whole idea of admiring themselves back on to you with comments such as, "What are you looking at? Don't you wish you looked this good?" Then they try to wink at you, as if. This physical and mental exacerbation has you, as the parent, wondering who in the hell has given my child a case of the five-hour energy pills when they should have given them a case of the five-hour shut-up.

As for the lying, anything and everything is a constant

topic of deniability. The familiar motives are, "Did you clean your bedroom," "Can you take out the trash," or "Can you feed the pets?" These are all met with an emphatic "Yes," of course. Later, when you ask if they have completed their chores, they just nod their head. But, when you walk by and observe their rooms, you'll see clothes on the floor along with magazines, video games scattered, and food that should be in the kitchen instead of on the floor and their beds. You realize this was a snow job, a pure fabrication and stretch of the truth. Not to mention the scout ants that are starting to see your teenager's rooms as the new pad in town. When you ask them about the overflowing trash can or the pets looking and begging for any type of food that a family member can spare. Their simple reply to the question of, "Did you do your chores?" is a golden, "Yeah, we did, didn't see the bed was made?" And you respond, "I did see your room with the blanket pulled over the bed, but I also saw the peculiar obstacles on the floor disguised as landmines in your bedroom. And there were some funny looking animal traps in there too." While you are telling them about all you observed, you gently bring up the fact that the animals were restlessly hungry and the trash was overflowing until you emptied it a few minutes earlier. They will swear they performed all their chores at some point in and around the time they were asked to do them, give or take a day or two.

Also, have you noticed a vocal, uncharacteristic display of behaviors that reminds you of an unbecoming, unfiltered five-year-old? They argue their point with such intensity and emotion. You would think they were moonlighting as either junior attorneys, English footballers, or thespians on a telenovela. You think to yourself, if they were on TV right now, they would be killin' it with all that acting, lying, and pleading. But they aren't. Surely you have witnessed the starting of conversations where you could not get a word in edgewise because you are dealing with a pseudo infantile boss who insists and thinks everyone works for them. If you are in such a conversation with them and decide to take sides on issues that are in disagreement with their views the conversation may end abruptly with, "You wouldn't even know because I'm so much smarter than you anyway. You can't even begin to contemplate what is in my brain." When they say things like this, my imagination runs wild with a picture of their brain being slowly sucked away into a blackhole due to the lack of oxygen to the brain and the lack of their infinite wisdom. This scenario might remind people of AMS, Acute Mountain Sickness, which occurs when normal people spend a lot of time exerting themselves at higher altitudes. Here they experience periods of confusion and not thinking straight. Teenagers, on the other hand, do this naturally without the mountain.

Furthermore, some teenagers suffering from this malady develop a love-hate relationship with other siblings that use the household territories. As we already know, sometimes it turns physical or it can just be the verbal jujitsu that always ends in "I didn't do it" or "I never said that." Sibling rivalry is ever so present at any age, young or old. Toshio Mori, in his classic Yokohama, California, details one such story that showcases the trials and tribulations of being kin. Mori's illustration is no different than any other sibling confrontation. It is about territory, tactics, and war. The two brothers, George and Tsuneo, were two years apart. The younger one (Tsuneo) is always vying for all that the older one (George) has. The problem started over an old desk that was George's. George loved the desk and had a great sense a pride for it. Thus, he placed all his possessions into the many drawers. The father, knowing that Tsuneo envied the desk, went out and bought him his own desk. For a time, everything seemed blissful, until Tsuneo felt George's desk carried more worth than his. Soon George began finding things missing in one drawer. Then, it spread to another and another. At first, George displayed a certain level of composure and restraint because he instinctively understood Sun Tzu's Art of War-to win the war you must lose some battles. While Tsuneo engaged in the tactic of attack and retreat. This is similar to the idea of picking at a scab. If you pick at a scab long enough it begins to bleed, and when it bleeds communication breaks down and war is declared. So, in all wars, blows are thrown. Here it is no different, except

Mom and Dad become very much like Jimmy Carter and Nelson Mandela brokering a peace deal.

3 PLANET ZIT

"Yes, I have bad skin. No, you don't need to
point it out to me."

~ Unknown ~

Another by-product of this stage is the manifestation of acne, which is the bumping of the skin. This bumping is precipitated by the overproduction of sebum, which clogs the pores of one's skin. Bacteria are then ensnared into these pores causing the protruding blemish, a.k.a. the pimple. The pimple is the name of a connoisseur's vernacular for acne.

Pimples are similar to ninjas or clear skin assassinators. One day, you're walking along enjoying your day snacking on some junk food and soda. Everything seems innocent, so you go home and watch TV. No problem! You decide to go to bed, but before you do you stop at the bathroom to brush your teeth. Soon after, you're taking a swig of mouthwash, gargling and spitting into the sink. You look up into the mirror and suddenly there it is, Apollo 11 on your nose. Girls tend to scream, and boys, well, they are still trying to be cool, looking into the mirror having a conversation with themselves. They say things such as, "C'mon, right now! Are you serious? Really!" Girls possibly follow up their scream with the following saying: "I can't go to school like this. I look like I just escaped from Planet Zit, and my nose was the only casualty."

When parents refuse to pay for the latest zit remover from TV's infomercials or let their teenager stay at home because of one or even a cluster of zits, the persistent teen usually will resort to using the only tools they have in their arsenal. This is either their phone or computer to access the internet, and thus begins their search for a natural or laboratory concoction that will eliminate or hide their untimely acne.

You know your teen has been in the bathroom preparing their pimple remedy due to the fact there is evidence on the mirror. The evidence appears to be toothpaste that may have been sprayed on the mirror when you are too close, and your mouth is open while brushing. But as you gaze at the mirror closely, you notice these objects are a creamy grayish-white. These specks are drizzled with crimson plasma veins running through them as if they were running down an erupting volcano. They are splattered all along the mirror and are the remnant of what is left from the pimple eruption that was caused by the pinching together of the two index fingers from the base of the opposing sides of each pimple located on your teen's face.

Thereafter, you begin to see traces of their newly formulated concoction on countertops, on the floor, and their face. In our house, it was aloe vera mixed with my spirulina protein power, which is expensive I might add. When you finally catch up with your teen they look like a small version of Marvel's Incredible Hulk. When you ask what is on their face, they say, "Don't ask, don't tell." I look over at my wife and say, "It works for me." This solution worked for me until I found out that little concoction clogged my sinks. Although this remedy turned out to be a halfway decent solution to my teen's acne issue, it wasn't the first attempt. The first attempt was using another internet search to find a solution. This time, the remedy involved toothpaste. Toothpaste was to be placed all over their face resembling a type of facemask. Then they are required to leave it on overnight to relieve their face of excess oil. An hour into this treatment, my teen started to experience a burning sensation all over their face as though their face was on fire. After the constant applying and rinsing of water, soap, and Noxzema relief was rendered, I had to remind my hormone-filled teen of the fact that not all things on the internet are true. Besides, I added, why don't you search for a more natural antidote rather than something chemically-based, thus, the systematic killing of the aloe plant and the reduction in my protein power.

Furthermore, related to the pimple cover-up, teenagers show their creativity in their attempt to lie in their discovery on the uses of the Band-Aid. For instance, when forced to go to school with a pimple protruding from their nose, they might say something along these lines: "My dog or cat scratched me that's why I have this Band-Aid on my nose." While their friends are thinking, "I never knew you had a dog or cat, and I've known you all my life. But if you say so."

4 THE GRAND NEGOTIATORS

"Everything is negotiable. Whether or not
negotiation is easy is another thing."

~ Carrie Fisher ~

Here, the swelling from the initial sting may have gone down, but the crazy's caused by it has stayed. As you already know or will find out, teenagers are very self-indulgent. They seek power and control of everything that includes their parents. Some parents give in and begin to follow their teenagers around subscribing to their beck and call. Another way of expressing this is learned helplessness. This gives rise to their false sense of security. When a teen is afflicted with this condition, parents contribute to their teen's delirium, agitation, lying, and action denial.

To combat these enigmas, I usually consult Robert Fisher and William Ury's book, *Getting to Yes: Negotiating Agreement Without Giving In.* This book gives parents a fighting chance in saving their rambunctious chemically-imbalanced infected teen rather than hindering them for life.

Teens are usually positional hard negotiators. A positional hard negotiator is someone who sees the environment and his or her relationships, either personal or interpersonal, as a contest of wills. Essentially, their way or the highway. For example, your teen girl may say something of the sort, "Mom, Dad, for my birthday, I want these types of clothes along with a big party at the skate center with all my friends, a cake, and a new phone. I know you are going to get these for me because if you don't, I'll be disappointed and you don't want that, right? Right!" As if it mattered in the first place. On the other hand, teenage boys may take this approach: "Dad, Mom, I know you going to get me those new trainers and hats because I'm already on the team you two told me to go out for and, of course, I made the team. The trainers and hat are quintessential items that will not only be suitable for my sport, but they allow me to have my style as an individual. Dad, you know what I'm talking about, right?" He slaps your hand to give you five followed by an immediate fist pump and then walks out of the room as if you agreed on something. You and your wife are left standing there looking at each other with bewilderment while pondering what just happened.

On the other hand, they see their parents as soft positional negotiators. A soft negotiator is a person who wants to avoid confrontation and conflict. So, a person who is considered a soft negotiator will seek concessions at the risk of being exploited to bring forth a resolution. For instance, parents may say that they cannot throw a big party, buy a cake, and take everyone to the skating center, but they will settle for Disneyland, Knott's Berry Farm, and or Magic Mountain as a concession.

Although the above methods of negotiations are prevalent, the more common approach a parent should and will use is the principled negotiation method. The principled negotiation method was derived from the Harvard Negotiation Project. When using this method, the chief negotiator elects to decide the issues or problems on their propositions rather than developing arguments that would and could give an advantage to each opposing side. It suggests the opposing members look for commonalities to resolve their differences. This method utilizes four precepts. Each precept focuses on a fundamental element of negotiation. They are people, interests, options, and criteria.

- When discussing issues about people, one must detach the issue from the person.

- Regarding interests, concentrate your efforts on their interests and yours.

- When considering options, create alternatives for mutual agreements.

- By the same token, when conversing on a standard of merit demand the use of objective criteria.

As a parent, that may be the way for some, but for me, I have a whole different type of approach. In a heated exchange, I want them to do what I want, when I want it, and how I want it. I simply refer to Abraham Maslow's hierarchy of needs, specifically level one and level two; physiological needs and safety needs. We provide the roof over their head as well as food, clothing, and a place to sleep. We also provide access to the internet, computers, dental, and medical. Also, the environment is safe to watch TV, do their homework, surf the web, and or just veg out in their rooms freely. Love, self-esteem, and self-actualization are contingent on successfully understanding and satisfying the needs of Mom and Dad.

5 PEER PRESSURE

"I'm not in this world to live up to your expectations and
your not in this world to live up to mine."

~ Bruce Lee ~

The dictionary defines peer pressure as a type of coercion
generated from one's social group, such as with teenagers.
Individuals feel they must act and perform actions deemed
acceptable by the group to fit in with other members of the
group. Frequently, I ask my teenager the million-dollar
question, "If there was a bridge, and your friends were
jumping off, would you?" His response would be, "How high
is the bridge?" So this just reinforces the point I'm trying to
make in this section. Peer pressure can and will affect your
teen's rational and coherent thought process. They will cease
to have their own identity, yet they'll claim they are acting in
defense of their individuality. For instance, teen boys on a
high school campus have no problem wearing the same
jacket, having the same haircut, wearing the same trainers,
pants, and shirt as their friends. They will move the same
way, dance the same way, and play the same sport. They will
talk in the same way and similarly have conversations with
others. For teen girls, their actions will undoubtedly be
identical to the boys without the wearing of the same

apparel. For teen girls, that crosses the line. They can have the same hairstyle and have the same earrings, but uniqueness in clothing choices is a must. If two girls show up wearing the same thing and it's not a school play or a performance, all hell will break loose. It will turn into a "Let go of my Eggo" moment. This means one of them will imply verbally and non-verbally to let go of the fashion no-no they are causing and go change immediately because you are not rockin' that outfit like I am. This will cause a rift in the friendship continuum. Depending on who is the better of the two in their negotiating skills will determine if the bond of sisterhood is dissolving.

Boys, on the other hand, if they showed up with the same outfit on would probably start to laugh, give each other compliments on their exquisite dapper fashion choices, and with the right music they would probably start break dancing in celebration of great minds think alike.

Although the above examples are somewhat comical, peer pressure can have negative domino effects on a teen's choice of friends, career, and life in general. It is the job of the parent to stay watchful and diligent regarding their impressionable teens because if you don't, what is the alternative? Drug addiction, depression, teen pregnancy, jail time, or even death. I as the parent, reserve the right to check rooms, computers, phones, and call the parents of other teens when I want and how I want. Random search and seizures of room and property will be at my discretion since I provide all the physiological needs and the security needs according to Maslow. Another way of saying this is, "My way or the highway."

6 BIRDS AND THE BEES

"My father told me all about the birds and the bees, the liar. I went steady with a woodpecker till I was twenty-one."

~ Bob Hope ~

Every spring, flowers erupt from their stems in an array of colors. During this season, one only has to breathe in deeply to smell the flowers, grass, and the air from the brisk rainstorms and the warming sun. The sun seems brighter, the sky bluer, and the clouds seem a little whiter than gray during this time of year. The days are longer and nights are shorter due to the earlier sunrises and later sunsets caused by the position of the sun as the earth rotates around it. In this period between March 19 through June 20th, you can easily observe the bees daily collecting pollen and nectar from the budding flower stamens to feed the colonies.

The birds have initiated their engagement into courtship. They begin a rhythmic synergic harmony that is sometimes vocal and seemingly dangerous to onlookers. This dance commences with a squaring off of the active participants: the male and female birds. They sometimes fly very high in the sky and then in a swirling freefall begin pecking at one another. Thereafter, they are flying in and out of different aerial pathways darting and dashing throughout the airways.

This action continues until the male solidifies his intention and the female accepts.

Similarly, birds are teenagers. In the spring, teenagers release their pheromonic signals and begin to square off competing for the opposing genders' affections. For the teen newbies, it starts with long stares at each other with the occasional smile and eye blinking. Then the female of the species hits the male, signaling the commencement of the courtship. Thus, begins the dance of the species. The male and female follow each other around all day in an attempt to invade the general proximity, inviting a telepathic dialogue with each other. At this stage, no words have been exchanged it is purely a non-verbal response. This action lingers on until one decides to involve a mutual negotiator, a person who can move in and out of each person's clique without causing a conundrum. This person will begin to ask questions of the two people as if they were on a particular game show. The first question being, "Like, do you have a boyfriend or girlfriend?" Once this is established, they can move on to the next round of inquiry. What is your Instagram hashtag? Are you on Twitter? Do you have YouTube Channel or TikTok account? After this series of questions have been answered, the teenagers start checking out their pages and posting likes and small messages to the contestants' personal sites. As a parent, you begin to see your teen's interest grow in the boy-meets-girl or the girl-meets-boy dramas, which were designed to be funny and comical, yet you can perceive your teenager looking at them with great focus and intent. This usually prompts the parent to say, "You know this is a movie, right? It isn't real life." Their response will almost be one hundred percent of the time, "I know." They will almost say anything to get you off their back, but you can see it in their faces and you can hear it in the little snicker they have while watching these types of television sitcoms. You as a parent are thinking to yourself, that wasn't funny at all. What are they chuckling about? Deep down you already know what is causing this imbalance—the birds and bees.

7 SOMEBODY ELSE'S PROBLEM

"The value of college education is not the
learning of many facts but the training
of the mind to think."

~ Albert Einstein ~

These days we're living purely as parent survivalists in a sink or swim environment. We are living in somewhat of a digital Vietnam or Iraq, where digital landmines, schemes, or propaganda can cause more damage to our impressionable teen's mind and reputation than what the insects could do. When you try to suggest to them the need to take a cybersecurity class, they respond by saying, "As if! I'm not a beginner, I know what I'm doing. Why don't you take it and tell me about it?" With that type of attitude, it pains me to want to help them, but being parents, we realize there's still a chance we can reach them on some level before they become drones of their sub-society. Their queen bee is the trendy trends online or reality celebrities that have little or no talent except questionable good looks, crazy hairdos, or a million followers spewing out the subliminal messages that relay information back to our teens. These messages pressure our teens to conform by relying on the other teen drones to act as surrogate role models to their queen bee model, the sub-society. If you start to notice subtle nuances that are out of the ordinary, such as lowered grades or a change in friends, break the glass on your parenting kit. First, take the phone and shut down their social networks and hashtags. Get your teen in touch with reality, insist they take part in an activity, club and/or tutoring, which is a part of the real world. Tell them they are not living in the Matrix, Ready Player One, or even the video game Tron. Assert that they live in a concrete jungle that calls for real social interaction. Convey to them this is needed for survival contrary to popular opinion. Inform them they will be going to college, passing an interview so they can get a job, and leaving your house one day in the future. Remind them, there will be no discussion on this matter. Let them know, "It is your way or the highway," due to the fact that you subscribe to Abraham Maslow's idea of psychology. Cue your teen in on the facts that you provide the roof over their head, food, clothing, a place to sleep, as well as access to the internet, computers, dental, and medical. Besides, emphasize that you as their parents provide a safe environment to watch TV, do their homework, and chores all while satisfying the needs of Mom and Dad.

Furthermore, tell them that until three things happen, they will be on perpetual probation where they will receive incremental privileges such as the usage of their phone, visitation, and outings with friends, and access to their social network with the caveat that big brother, a.k.a. Mom and Dad, will be watching. Convey to your teenager, probation is contingent on first, grade improvement, and secondly, all new friends need to be introduced to you. The third thing that has to happen is a complete unequivocal acknowledgment and understanding of the expectations outlined in the first two guidelines. Once these three conditions are met, they will be granted conditional probation and be allowed privileges to possess their phone again, plus visitation rights will be subsequently restored as well as access to social networks. Probation will last for a 2-3-year term, whereupon they will be granted full rights of the household again, but by then they will be somebody else's.

THE SYNDROME

8 THE EPILOGUE

FRESHMEN 15

Friendship is unnecessary, like philosophy, like art... It has no survival value; rather it is one of those things that give value to survival.

~ C.S. Lewis

When your son or daughter is delivered to an institution of higher learning, parents seem to relish the idea of an empty nest or a one child two parent household. S.Q.T. or Spousal Quality Time is just a click or a phone call away especially in the summer when you can send the other child to camp for weeks. Just the thought of being able to gaze into the fireplace with your significant other without the usual stampede bursting in as you pour an adult refreshment into a glass and asking about how many smores are you going to make? What movie are we going to watch? Or, are you going to do that Jiffy Pop thing over the fire?

I often ponder the line from The Godfather III, when Michal Corleone states, "Just when I thought I was out, they pull me back," as the case with my notorious son. After living abroad, not overseas, but just out of my house for a quarter, the holidays arrived along with my son. He was almost unrecognizable. When he left for university, he was tall, lanky, and fit due to his habitual on demand exercise regimen courtesy of Shaun T's Insanity. When my wife and I arrived at the university's commons to pick him up, he was unshaven, his hair in disarray, and his mid-section had grown a tad. Also, just adjacent to his being was a ton of laundry in my old Army duffle bag with two baskets of dirty laundry behind it. As if that wasn't a site, some young hipster wearing Daisy Duke shorts, a tank top, and a fall jacket walks up to him. Then, she holds his hands, puts them behind her waist and plants a sloppy kiss on him all while we are walking up to greet him. My wife shouted, "That's my son!" The girl turns and says, "I know. He's cute, isn't he?" Stooped, and totally taken off guard by her comment, my wife looks at me in desperation. I throw my arms up and shake my head to signify I have no idea or explanation of what just occurred only to tell her it lasted about 20-30 seconds. She was irked by my comment and went on to state that I was lucky that our daughter chose to visit a friend today rather than take the ride to pick up her brother. Otherwise, she would have witnessed that little brazen hussy and her actions. She would have probably had the impression that prancing around half naked in the fall kissing a boy like a marathoner races was what you did in college.

I thought to myself, it wouldn't be long before we're in the thick of things again with my daughter. The venom was already in her bloodstream and was beginning to catalyze with her hormones that were being released from her hypothalamus. I can see the "it" rising within her, the monster that was and will be again on the threshold of life, as the cycle continues.

As I snap out of my walking daydream, I realized my wife and I are standing in front of our underclassmen son and his female companion. I shake his extend hand and say, "Good afternoon son, how are you," and then give him a hug. His mother extends her hand and some polite courtesies to Ms. So and So, while grimacing. It really didn't matter what her name was, but it was gut wrenching watching my wife will her way through the salutations and pleasantries, like drinking coffee with the grinds. As my son's female companion informed us, she had to leave, due to the fact she saw her parents arriving. So, she ever so smoothly walks away turning her head to catch our gaze and says, "I'll see you in about a week and half?" My wife started immediately doing the calculations coming up with the answer to this unorthodox word problem, and stated, "That's Christmas!" My son, uttered," Oh yeah! I invited her over for Christmas." "You did what?" my wife responded. "We'll get through it. It will be ok, you'll see." I conveyed to her. Thereafter, my son motioned to hug his mother and gave her a kiss. She abruptly interrupted him, and said, hold on a second. She opened her purse and handed him her emergency travel-size mouthwash. Gargle first, before you kiss your mother. I don't want to come down with any type of college disease from little Ms. Communicable.

The car ride home should have been filled with inquiries about his first quarter in college but one topic seemed to dominate the discussion. Who is she, where is she from, what is her nationality, and so on? The top question of the day revolved around status. I asked my son, is she your girlfriend? He replied, we're not really in to titles. We kind of have this thang and we are seeing where it takes us. This thang, it's mono y mono right, my wife inferred. My son just repeated, we are just hanging out. "It sounds like the free love of the 60's," I replied. My son uttered, "yup!" I informed him at some point you are going to have to commit and learn to lead. Notice there are no more flower children or the so-called hippies. They all had to grow up, face the music, and take some responsibility for their lives. My son immediately looked over at me and asked, "Are you preaching to me already?" "No son, I'm not. I'm just stating the obvious. Nietzsche once said, there are no facts, only interpretations. Well, it's clear to me why they do not exist anymore and why your mother and I have a mortgage, two kids, and a relationship that spans more than two decades. Is that existential enough for you?" "Preach it! Preach it, brother preach it," my wife exclaimed. My son just grinned, looked down at the car floor and shook his head. I took a look up at him via the rear-view mirror, then voiced, for the rest of the car ride, let's keep it light, as I turned on the radio.

A few days after my wife completed washing all my son's dirty clothes, he asked if we would buy him some snack food for his dorm. So, my wife took him to market. We still couldn't wrap our heads around the endless amount of Top Ramen, economy size spaghetti and pasta sauces, and Spam he wanted. After maneuvering through the food aisles, he casually walked the feminine needs aisle stopping in front of the prophylactic section. My wife asked him, "What do you think you are doing?" He replied, nonchalantly, that he was looking for his brand and they seemed to be out of it. He then proceeded to walk on, unphased and unperturbed by the question like he was some type of stud. As if? That would be the day. Only if we are talking horses and donkeys of course.

A few days later, he informed us that he needed to visit the doctor, due to his ailing wrist. So, we obliged and took him. The doctor evaluated him, acknowledged the freshmen 15-pound weight gain and then diagnosed him with Carpal tunnel and gave him an arm-wrist brace to wear. He informed us he must have developed it from either typing and or writing all those notes in class sessions. His mother and the doctor were buying that nonsense, hook, line, and sinker. I had another theory. Ever since my son has been home, he has been participating in these all-night gaming events. Waking up late and going to bed around 4 am in the morning. In addition, he has been eating an insurmountable amount of cheese puffs to go along with the swearing and laughter he put forth to video characters on the TV screen after 1 am. Now the doctor went ahead and gave him an arm-wrist brace so he would be comforted rather than strained when playing e-sports. With his unshaven face, he now resembled a blood shot eyed 1970's G.I. Joe with Kung Fu grip zombie toy with cheese powder all over his hands, face, and game controller. I was not even sure he was coherent in this post symbiotic state. At this point, he was just existing, breathing in and breathing out, putting more strain on his heart with his freshmen 15.

CHRISTMAS DINNER

You can tell a lot about a person by the way they handle
three things; a rainy day, lost luggage, and
tangled Christmas lights.

~ Maya Angelou

For most of us, Christmas is a time shared and reserved for
the giddy gift giving spectacle amongst children and their
families. This happy occasion is somewhat interrupted with a
shot of stress and a side of anxiety when a child goes off to
college and returns on break. This is due to the remote
chance their offspring would go off an invite a friend of the
opposite sex to take part in the family's traditions and
festivities. Call it kismet or happenstance, suddenly you
have an individual at your door without a monkey's paw to
remedy the situation. The wife at the juncture has resorted to
using the evil eye on everyone so, the festive atmosphere
around cooking, baking, and singing with holiday cheer is all
but diminished. The fathers are usually the one's to try to
break the code of silence and tension by making comments
such as, it's going to be okay, just calm down, and or relax, it
just a few hours. To Mom's, those words although coming
from their significant other represent empty promises.
Mom's will go into full beast mode to keep up appearances
and cordiality at all cost. In their eyes they have their dignity

to uphold and if the dinner doesn't go as planned, they still have the sacredness of New Year's Day dinner.

In our particular scenario, the honored guest arrived in a well-tailored form fitting holiday dress that came down to her thigh. It was black, with sequins, chiffon on the arms. Also, she wore a soft red lip stick with just right amount of blush and eyeliner. In addition, she wore her hair in a bun with a red Japanese style Kanzashi hair ornament with matching heeled sandals. My son was in awe of her striking beauty. His mouth was open, his voice was fumbling for words, so as the man of the house I said, "Come in, welcome." It was like he had never seen her in this particular light before. He gave her a slight kiss on the cheek, while his sister giggled staring with amazement. We all lined up and stood at the door introducing ourselves and giving her greetings and salutations. Thereafter, we sat around the family table playing board games, listening to music, and telling exaggerated stories while we waited for dinner to be served. The tension seemed to have dissipated, due to the girl's new found demeanor and tact. Without noticing, the elephant in the room seemingly had left the holiday dinner where it had presided all day long. Finally, everything was going seemingly well, the girl was getting along with everyone including my wife. The tribe had harmoniously accepted her presence, at least that's what I thought.

Out of nowhere the girl, the invited guest, informed everyone she had an announcement to make. My wife's mind started to swirl and became very anxious about the situation. Her face rapidly became very pale in color. As the guest started to speak, my wife began to blurt out answers, presumably her worst fears realized, such as, "Are you pregnant?" "Are you two getting married?" as if she was a contestant on the game shows Jeopardy and or the Wheel of Fortune.

Immediately after, I felt the blood rushing into my face from embarrassment, and I could hear that symbolic elephant stampeding back into the room. No! The girl emphatically responded to both questions. I just wanted to invite you all to New Year's Day brunch at my house. Well it took a second or two to process but we all exhaled and laughed with a sigh of relief after my wife put everyone on high ready alert one with her comments. Thereafter, I took my wife over to the mini bar, poured her and I a drink and toasted the evening. Then we graciously walked over to the honored guest and accepted her invitation to join her family for New Year's Day brunch.

END.

AUTHOR'S PAGE

Mark Adkins is a devoted husband, father of two, and part-time author at large. He enjoys sketching, painting, as well as, spending time riding the waves and eating tacos at the beach.

If you would like to leave a review, comment, and or question for either of Mark's books, please log on to **www. easywritor.com**. Also, at **easywritor.com** you can find about his latest projects and favorite tacos dives.

The proceeds from the books go directly to Mark's pursuit of a Doctorate of Philosophy (PhD.). Graduate school is expensive. So, if you can be a gifter, buy three, keep one and give two away as gifts. Mahalo!

www.ingramcontent.com/pod-product-compliance
Lightning Source LLC
Chambersburg PA
CBHW071754020426
42331CB00008B/2307